CW00925426

LAKE DISTRICT
DIALECT

A selection of words and anecdotes
from around The Lake District

by
Lucy Thirlmere

BRADWELL
BOOKS

Published by Bradwell Books
9 Orgreave Close Sheffield S13 9NP
Email: books@bradwellbooks.co.uk

All rights reserved. No part of this publication may be
produced, stored in a retrieval system or transmitted
in any form or by any means, electronic, mechanical,
photocopying, recording or otherwise without the prior
permission of Bradwell Books.

British Library Cataloguing in Publication Data:
a catalogue record for this book is available from
the British Library.

1st Edition

ISBN: 9781910551165

Print: Gomer Press, Llandysul, Ceredigion SA44 4JL

Design and artwork by: Andrew Caffrey

Photograph Credits: iStock, Creative Commons and
Cumbria Image Bank. Images credited separately.

Introduction

Is dialect more about a place's past or its present? When it comes to the Lake District and Cumbria, it's very much about both. These parts of the country are fortunate to have many champions and a lively passion for local words, phrases and pronunciation, making them alive with their own distinctive language.

When most of us think about words and the Lake District, we think of WORDSWORTH and BEATRIX POTTER. While these figures made an important contribution to the perception of the place, the links between place and language are even richer and more varied than this. Cumbria boasts a proud heritage of dialect writers, a line of people from all walks of life who made sure that the words that they heard in their day (and before) were celebrated.

In *The Stories of English*, DAVID CRYSTAL comments that, in the past, *'Dialects were not usually viewed as a living medium of expression, offering a window into cultural diversity; rather they were thought of as relics of past times, quaint curiosities to be cherished and preserved.'*

In contrast with this, in Lakeland and Cumbria, as this book explores, there are clear signs that the local dialects are not simply fascinating parts of the past, but living languages still very much in use. There is no doubt that many of the words and sayings featured in our glossary are no longer part of everyday life, but some of them certainly still are. The continuing line of local dialect writers in the area also shows that the dialects of Cumbria are alive rather than just preserved. Even the response to Cumbria's rapping farmer shows that the dialect is alive and that public interest in it is too!

Sadly, there is only time in this short book to look at the subject in brief. Enthusiasts keen for more will find plenty to explore locally and in person. Whether you're taking a peek at the way local people referred to their working life, or looking at legendary tales of the area or the varied industries that have connections with the place, one thing is clear: there's a great deal more to the Lake District than Wordsworth and his celebrated daffodils. But dialects don't stand still. Neither do places. Like everywhere else, the Lake District is affected by commercial developments and other forces around it. While there's no denying that the area is currently going through change, its identity will always be closely associated with the words and language of its people.

Glossary

ANIMALS

Bessie dooker – water bird

Bield – a windbreak on the fells, usually a length of wall with two sides of a square

Borran – foxhole or rabbit warren

Brock – a badger

Correct – used to describe when an animal is in good condition at a sale

Cowt – colt

Crowdy – a type of porridge for animals

Crackets – crickets

Crag fast – when a sheep has become stuck on a ledge on a crag

Gowk – a cuckoo, or a thoughtless person who talks too much about one subject

Heaf – a portion of fell where a flock always grazes

Heafed – a flock that knows its own heaf or portion of fell

Heronsue – heron

Hogg – young sheep in the stage between weaning and first shearing, between 5 and 14 months old

Hoggest – corruption of *hoggus* or *hogg-house*, a place young sheep used to shelter in severe weather during their first winter

Horn-burn – initials burned onto an animal's horn as means of identification

Ketmar – tern

Kye – cows

Midge/n – house fly

Miller's thumb – willow wren

Mowdy-(warp) – mole

Mowdy-tump – mole-hill

Naigs – horses

Nowt – cattle

Rattens – rats

Throssle – a thrush

Varmen or varmint – vermin

Whye – a heifer

Yad – a mare

CLOTHES

Brat – apron

Breeks – breeches

Claes – clothes

Cleed – to clothe

Clip and heel'd – properly dressed

Doff – to undress

Don – to dress

Duds – coarse clothes

Furbellows – fancy silks, frills

Kitle – thin jacket

Leace – lace

Mid-thie – mid-thigh

Mittens – gloves

Sark – shirt

Trinkums – useless finery

FARMING

Lunchtime during harvest in Brigsteer, Kendal in 1898 Cumbrian Image Bank

Braffam – horse collar

Byre – cow-house

Car – cart

Carras – a shade or cart-house

Clippers – sheep shears or the shearers themselves

Clipping oot – removing dirty wool from round the tail

Cock – a small cone-shaped pile of hay left to dry in a hay field

Cwoley – a farmer's or shepherd's dog

Dogging – to use dogs to drive another farmer's stock away to different ground

Faul – farm-yard

Gear – wealth, money, or the tackling of a cart or plough

Greype – a three-pronged instrument used to clean cow-houses

Hlaup – the first milk after calving

Kye – cows

Kyeak'n – feeding sheep with 'cake' or concentrate food before and after lambing to encourage the milk flow

Laird – a farmer's eldest son or person who possesses land

Pleugh – plough

Shearin – reaping

Nowt – cattle

Whye – a heifer

FOOD

Ambrie – pantry

Bait/Bate – sandwiches

Bannocks – bread made of oatmeal

Buits – boots

Butter-shag – a slice of bread spread with butter

Butter-sops – wheat or oat bread, soaked in melted butter and sugar

Cabbish – cabbage

Ceake – cake

Ceyder – cider

Cow'd-lword – a pudding made of oatmeal and suet

Cruds – curds

Dubbler – a wooden platter

Gurdle – the iron on which cakes are baked

Havver – oats

Hinney – honey

Keak – cake

Keale – broth

Poddish – pottage

Schuil – school

Scons – cakes made of barley meal

Scotty kye – Highland cattle

Shwort-cakes – rich fruit cakes

Snaps – small round gingerbread cakes

Sour-milk – butter-milk

Spuin – spoon

Wots – oats

Yell – ale

HOME

Backseyde – the yard behind a house

Bellasis – bellows

Chimley – chimney

A view of Carlisle's Castle Street in 1895 Cumbria Image Bank

Clemmed – hungry or cold

Coppy – small stool

Croft – a field behind the house

Duir – door

Fluir/fleer – floor

Knop – a large tub

Latch – a wooden sneck

Loft – the upper apartment of a cottage

Menseful – hospitable, generous

Neybor – neighbour

Nuik – nook

Onset – dwelling-house and outbuildings

Piggen – a wooden dish

Sampleth – sampler

Sarra – to serve

Sattle – a long seat

Seape – soap

Steeyul – stool

Sticks – furniture

Stuil – stool

Teable – table

Wun – to dwell

Catching up at the Mardale Shepherds Meet in 1954 Cumbria Image Bank

NATURE

Beck – stream

Booins – ragwort or groundsel

Breer – briar

Clart – sticky muck

Cleg – horse fly

Creyke – creek

Croft – a field behind the house

Daggy – drizzly

Deyke – hedge

Dockin – dock plant

Dub – pool in a stream

Eshes – ash-trees

Fell – mountain

Greymin – a thin covering of snow

Ketlock – wild mustard

Kingcup – marsh marigold

Muin – moon

Muir – moor

Paddock rud – frog spawn

Ruse – rose

Seugh – ditch

Sleas – sloes

Stank – weir or floodgate

Syke – a small stream

Tarn – a small lake or any small pool of water

PEOPLE

Bogie – a ghost or apparition

Cobbed – peculiar

Doo – a social occasion

Dowly – unwell

Ee – eye

Een – eyes

Feace – face

Fratch – quarrel, to quarrel

Freeten'd – frightened

Freet – to grieve

Gob – mouth

Gowl – to weep

Granfadder – grandfather

Granson – grandson

Head-wark – headache

Hether-fac'd – rough-faced

Howdey – a midwife

Jaw – mouth

Kith – acquaintances

Lanlword – landlord

Leady – lady

Leame – lame

Leet – to meet with, to alight

Lissen – to listen

Lugs – ears

Luive – love

Maffle – to blunder, to mislead

Maister – master

Mant – to stutter

Mazle – to wander about in a dazed state

Mudder – mother

Pate – head

Paughty – proud, haughty

Paut – to walk heavily

Pawky – shy, too familiar

Pech – to pant

Peer – poor

Pleenin – complaining

Potticary – apothecary

Rievers – border robbers

Sarvant – servant

Seypers – immoderate drinkers

Thoum – thumb

Thropple – windpipe

Titty – sister

PLAY

Cairds – cards

Diddle – to hum a tune

Dissnins – a distance in horse-racing

Dook – swim

Flyre – to laugh

Gamlers – gamblers

Kettelt – kettled, under the influence of alcohol

Kittle – to tickle

Laik – to play

Lant – a game of cards

Pops and pairs – a card game

Russlin – wrestling

Whornpeype – hornpipe

The Whitehaven pet goose, pictured with fans and admirers in 1910

Cumbrian Image Bank

The story goes that Barney the goose was originally imported to Whitehaven from Ireland but escaped his fate because he was too thin! He ended up living in the local marketplace with Billy Bell and his family in 1900. Barney became a familiar sight in Whitehaven and was given treats at regular haunts around the town. His favourite food was said to be bread dipped in beer! Barney the goose lives on at Whitehaven harbour to this day with the name being given to any goose that decides to live in the area!

WORK
Cleek – to catch with a hook
Darrak – a day's labour
Durdem – broil
Dust, durdem – money
Deetin – winnowing corn
Gully – a large knife
Kurn – to churn
Lapstone – a shoemaker's stone
Michael – hemp cord for tying sheaves
Prent – print
Reape – rope
Shoul – shovel
Smiddy – smithy
Stee – ladder
Teaylear/tealyor – tailor
Wark – work
Weage – wage

From *A Supplement to the Glossary of the Dialect of Cumberland* by E.W. PREVOST, published 1905

Similes current in the county

Badly used like a dolly-tub bottom

Bad-tempered as nettles

Bald as a bledder o' saim

Bare as a bald heed

Bent as a sickle

Big as a mill-wheel

Black as a crow

Blinnd as a bat

Blue as a leah steann

Blue as wad (woad)

Blue as whinsteann

Blunt as my grandmudder knees (of a knife)

Bonny as a sheep kead (sarcastic)

Brankan' like a steg swan

Brant as a bawk-stee

Brant as a besom

Brant as a pump

Brazzant as a yerd o pump watter

Breet as a bald heed

Breet as a bullace

Breet as a nip

Breet as a seeing glass

Bumman aboot like a bee in a bottle

Busy as inkle weavers

Catching as t' mizzles

Catching as t' scab

Cheap as muck and twice as nasty

Clean as a wizzel

Cloggy as a fat su'

Coald as a geavlick (of a piercing draught through a hole or window)

Coald as ice (as charity)

Common as brackens

Common as a sneck (used by all)

Conceited as a banty-cock

Crabb't as a cuckoo

Cracked as a brokken (keal) pot

Creuk't as acammeral

Creuk't as a dog's hind leg

Creuk't as a grunstean hannel

Creuk't as a sickle

Cruel as an atter (spider)

Daft as besoms

Daft as a cuddy

Daft as a geuse nick't i' t'heed

Daft as a gurse-gaan gezlin

Daft as a yet 'at oppens beath ways

Dancen like a steg on a het gurdle

Dark as Oald Nick's nuttin pwoke

Dark as a pwoke

Deed as a deer nail

Deed as a dockin

Deed as a hammer

Deed as a herrin'

Deed as a mawky rattan

Deed as a nippen

Deed as a teadd skin

Deef as a deef cuddy

Deef as a post

Deef as a steann

Dowly as a pawnshop

Drunk as cloy

Drunk as a fiddler

Drunk as muck

Drunk as a potter (the last stage of drunkenness)

Dry as bass (of hay)

Dry as bones (of corn)

Dry as caff

Dry as dust

Dry as a limekiln (of a very thirsty person)

Dry as a sandbed (of a thirsty man)

Dry as snuff (of hay)

Dull as a dolly-stick

Dusty as a flooar pwoke

Fast as a grosser cutten butter

Fast as hen pickan bigg

Fast as a rebbat

Fat as a bull

Fat as butter

Fat as a con

Fat as a tailor's geuse

Fat as mawks

Femmer as a spider wob

Fond as a brush

Fond as a yet 'at oppens beath ways

Friendly as a black-kite bush

Friendly as yan's shadda

Froff as a carrot

Full as an egg is of meat

Full as a fitch

Game as a cockroach

Gangan like a steg wi egg

Geud-nater't as a pump

Grand as a steany

Greedy as a reak

Handy as a kitten (of a well-mannered horse)

Hard as a beck steann (very obstinate)

Hard as brazzle

Hard as a fell teadd

Hard(y) as ling

Hard as nails

Hard as an otter

Hee as a steeple

Heeds an' thraws like Jock an' his mither

Het as fire

Ill-gien as oald Nick's nuttin' bag

Kaim't as a tup whom

Kaykan aboot like a pet geuse

Keen as a geavlick (of a piercing draught through a window or hole)

Kittle as a moose

Kittle as a moosetrap

Aw knots, like a Keskadale yak

Laal set be as muck

Laal thowt on as dyke watter

Laal wantit as rain i' hay time

Lang as a fiddle

Lang as a priest cwoat

Lang as Souter leath corner (very long)

Lang as a wet seek

Lazy as he's lang

Lazy as a pig

Lazy as a stee

Leam as a three-legged dog

Lean as a harrow

Lean as a reak

Leeks as a basket

Leet as caff

Leet as a fedder (as a cleckin)

Leet as a fleea (as a lop)

Leet as a midge

Fresh air and exercise at Bishop Goodwin School in 1924

Cumbria Image Bank

Lennok as a wet shirt

Limp as a dishcloot

Lish as a bullock

Lish as a cat

Lish as a four (two)-year old (of a horse)

Lish as a squirrel

Lively as a crakket

Lively as a hawk

Lonely as a mile-steann

Lowse as a pump hannel

Mad as a bull at a yet

Mad as a piper

Mad as a poo't swine

Mean as dirt

Mucky as a dub (duckpond)

Mucky as t' grun'

Mum as a moose

Munjan an' creunan' like a bull at a yet

Neak't as a heedsteann

Nice (dainty) as an otter

Nimmel as a cat

Noisy as a tinkler

Oald as the fells

Oald as granfadder hat

Oald as Knock-cross

Oald as Walker broo (Workington)

Oppen as a riddle

Peer as a kirk moose

Peert as a pyet

Plain as a pikestaff

Plain as a yet stoop

Pricky as an urchin

Pubble as a partridge

Raffy as a tinkler

Ram as a fox

Ram as an oald Billy gwoat

Rank as mice in a meal kist

Rank as nettles

Reed as the chollers of a bubbly-jock

Reed as a fox

Reed as a herrin'

Reet as a bobbin (as a trivet)

Roon' as a bullet

Rough as hedder

Rowtin like a quey in a fremd lonnin (said of a boisterous man)

Sad as bull's liver

Sare as a kyle

Scabbt as a cuckoo

Sharp as a breear

Sharp as a gimlick (of bright eyes)

Sharp as leetnin'

Sharp as a sheep keadd

Sharp as whins

Sharp as a wizzel

Slab as butter

Slape as an ackron

Slape as an eel

Slape as an eel tail greased

Slape as a greasy pole

Slape as a needle

Slo' as a sneel

Smart as a carrot with jags on

Snell as a stepmudder breeth

Snod as a mowdywarp

Soft as muck

Soft as pap

Soft as a turmet

Soft-hear tit as a wizzel

Soond as a drum (of deep sleep)

To stick like a cleg

Stink like a foomart

Strang as a bull (as a horse)

Strang as an onion

Strang as rotten cheese

Strang as a yak

Street as a dog's hind leg

Street as a resh (as a seeve)

Street as truth

Street as a wan'

Street as a yerd o' pump watter

Suer as a gun

Swak as an eel

Sweerin' like a tinkler

Sweet as a kern (as a nut)

Sweet as botcher

Teugh as fig-fag

Teugh as (shoe) ledder

Teugh as pinwire

Teugh as a soople

Teugh as wax

Thick as inkle weavers

Thin as a cat lug

Thin as a lat

Thin as a milkin-steul leg

Thin as a shadda'

Thrang as a bummely

Thrang as fleuks in a sheep liver

Thrang as inkle weavers

Thrang as three in a bed

Thrang as Throp wife

Tight as a drum

Tight as wax

Tired as a dog

Wake as dish watter

Wake as a kitten

Wake as a teufet

Wake as waiter

Wake as a winnelstrea

Wankle as a seek

Wankle as a wet pwoke

War ner seut

Warm as toast

Welsh (wairsh) as pump watter

Wet as a dishcloot

Wet as draif

Wet as a duck

Wet as a fish

Wet as pash (poss)

Wet as sump

Wet as thack

Whick as an eel

Whick as a lop

Whisht as a cat

Whisht as a moose

Whisht as yan's shadda'

White as a ghost

Wild as winter thunner

Yalla as a gowan

Proverbs, proverbial expressions and phrases

Auld keall ur seuner warm't ner new 'uns meade – alludes to the renewal of an old courtship

Wink at yowe an' worry't lamb – to be deceitful and take every advantage

Theer nowte seah queer as fwoke

A cat canna fare weel an' lane

Eoon aboot for t' bainest

Buy a horse wi' a weamm an' a mear wi' neann

When t' whin's oot o' blossom, kissin's oot o' fashin

Owt'u mak a parson?

Feckless fwok are aye fain

Whedder cum tittermest – whoever comes first; first come, first served

Jolly neets mak sworry mworns

Seldom cu' t' better – change is not always an improvement

Niver say nowt bit laif

T' back en's oalas t' bare en'

Aback o' beyont whoar t' meer fwoaled t' fiddler

Slivan gangs wi' t' bait

Geap gorbie an' thoo'll git a worm

Let that hare sit – said when an unkind tale is being told, or when one man is running another down

Maidens' barns are aye weel bred

Mair clout ner pudden

Change is leetsom if it's nobbut oot o' bed intill beck

Better a wee buss than neah beeld

If the sheep can get a mosscrop a day, they'll do with a foddering less of hay

Bed-time for berriers an' supper-time for carriers

A blate cat maks a prood moose

It's a dree rwoad 'at hes niver a turn

If ther wer neah fells ther'd be neah dells

Niver use the taws when a gloom will do as well

A haw year, a snaw year

Dum fwok heirs neah lan'

Where the lamb sucks there it will be – refers to the Herdwick sheep, which stays in the area in which it was born

Nowt niver taks neah harm

Nowt hes neah heamm

Nowt's niver i' danger

Better flaitch a feul ner feight him

A woman'll thrive whoar a man cannut fend

Many a hen can sit 'at canna flee – implies that at times it is best to act against one's wishes in case a worse thing happens to you

Yan's tied teh lig as yan's bigged

Ken yersel an' yer neebours'll nut misken yeh

A green year's as bad as a shak – to do anything too soon is often as bad as doing it too late

Lonterin' fwok's oalas lazy fwok

Shinny's weel enough if shins wer' seaff

Plenty o' butter wad sto' a dog

A lad ageann neunn an' a lass ageann neet – refers to the proper time at which the farm servants should come home

Thar's lile difference atween mense and sham – there is only a step between decorum and shame

Of a cold day: **fit to starve a geavlick**

Of a noisy eater: **he gaas munchin' an' slobberin' on at his meat liker a swine routin' apples in a pail o' wesh ner owt else**

Of a full fine eye in a horse: **an eye in his heed fit to kinnel a whin buss**

Of a horse that forges: **he plays hammer an' tangs**

Of a cold-shouldered horse: **he would not pu' a docker off her nest**

Of a keen active-going horse: **he'll scraffle up t' brantest broo liker a tarrier ner owt else**

Of a horse which has the trick of occasionally (or oftener) kicking: **he's leet ahint**

When harrows begin to hop, cannel leet mun stop

When Scotch fwok starts to pu' their geese, it's teyme

to hoose baith nags an' beese

Efter oald Cannelmas neet, keukks finnd cannel leet

When t' burr's far t' rains' nar

A far-off burr tells of a narhand storm

Mair din ner dow – more noise than work

Mair luck an less fash – a toast at social gatherings

Of a lazy man: **he's yen o thur Cum-day-gang-day-God-send-Sunday kin' o' chaps**

A cum-day-gang-day body maks neah provision

A lazy man disinclined for exercise will excuse himself on the ground that he **'he's a beann in his leg'**

A man who has married for money has **'weddit t' midden for't sake o't muck'**

A widower who marries soon after his wife's death may be told that **'a beelen coo seunest fergits t' cofe'**

A man may be **'that drunk 'at he canna see a whol in a stee'** or can **'nowder stan', sit, ner hod be t' gurse'**

After a night's spree a man is said to **'cheg dog-gurse'**

A lucky man is like a cat – **'he oalas fa's ov his feet'**

Of a man having an unquenchable thirst: **he is a fair sandbed for drink**

Of one at all times ready for a drink: **his throat's middlen slippy**

Of one whose red and blotched face tells a tale of steady drinking: **he's pentit his feace till some teunn**

I'o keep doon t' form-heed – to take a nap after dinner

To be sent to **Durdar Docks** or **Bleckell Cheese Quarries** – to be sent on a fool's errand

A blacksmith's calling is '**a drooty (drufty)** trade'

A smiddy's a gay drufty spot – alludes to the reputed drunken habits of smiths

Food cut very thin '**smells of the knife**'

A mortgagee is referred to as '**sitten astride o' t' riggin**'

Inquiry as to whether there is a mortgage on a property may be made in the following terms: **Anybody leukin' oot o' t' chimley? Anybody sitten astriddlen o' t' riggin? Is it gayly sair dipped? Is ther a monkey on't riggin?**

Nut to care a button top – implies complete indifference

Of a sharp-featured person – **his nwose wad split a hailsteann**

Of a short and stout person – **yen o' Bob Wilkin mak, a stiff an' thick un**

A short person will be told to '**jump up an' nep a daisy**'

Of a snub-nose – **wad deuh fer a hat creukk**

A sick person who makes no progress either one way or other '**neither dees ner dows**'

To have a needle into any one – to have a spite against a person

A person uncouth in gait **'waddles leyke a duck wid egg'**

Of one unable to make a good meal: **he's nowther fuller ner fainer**

Of a difficult thing: **it caps a fleukk** (which is slippery in the hand)

A reticent person, or one depressed in mind, or having no powers of conversation, **'hesn't a word te fling till a dog'**

Those who are subject to a great variety of temper will be said to be **'Owder** *(ower t'; ower t'; at t'; in t')* **meunn**, or *(t'; doon in't; t'; in't)* **midden**

Yan's seah like tudder yeh canna tell wedder tudder's which

Yan's so like tudder at yan cannut tell thro' tudder's which

A witless person **'hes the sense ov a sookan turkey'**

Of a strong wind – **fit to skin a paddock (teadd)**

Of a strong wind – **fit to blow t' diwel's whorns off him**

Of one who is suspected of shamming sickness – **he'd be war if he ail'd owt**

Theer mair fwoke gits weddit nor can boil t' pot on Sunday

To git t' wrang pig be't lug – implies an error made by someone

Nin can say black's me nail

Off yan's eggs an' on ta laal taties – implies the folly of waste efforts, as when a hen sits without any eggs under her

She'll leuk at riders till fit-fwok gan by – a variant of the preceding

He's nin but a judcock 'at maks hay in October, an' a gowk 'at sows havver when t' cuckoo's com over

Ah's gan yam – I'm going home

Werst thew of te? – Where are you going?

Fine fettal – Good health

Hod thee whish't – Be quiet

It'll be reet – It will be alright

Oust fettal? – How are you?

Haig Colliery Mike Jackson

THE LAKE DISTRICT DIALECT

A little word about place

In the past, the Lake District was divided between the areas of **Westmorland, Cumberland** and **Lancashire**. Now it is fully in the county of Cumbria. For the purposes of this short book, we explore the dialects of the Lake District and Cumbria.

How do you pronounce Cumbrian?

As you would expect, Cumbrian and Lake District accents vary throughout the region. However, they do have some general rules in common. One of these is that if you're referring to something, you will usually shorten it to '*t*'. As you might guess if you've heard Cumbrians speak, the vowel sounds are very similar to Northern vowels. If you're using a word with the '*oo*' in it, you should pronounce it as if it has a '*y*' in it, for example, '*cool*' is pronounced as '*cyel*'. Another pattern is that the '*y*' sound is added to words with a long '*a*', for example '*cake*' becomes '*cyak*'.

However, as with every dialect, there are exceptions to these rules. It's one thing to read about the Cumbrian accent, but another to listen to it! To hear people speaking in the local accent, visit the British Library website at: **http://sounds.bl.uk/Accents-and-dialects**

On the dialect

There are shades and variations of pronunciation and accent in the districtal dialects which are extremely difficult to explain; and which can only be properly understood on hearing the native speakers in unrestrained colloquial glee, or in angry recrimination.

The strangeness of some words and expressions cannot be duly estimated from the sound alone, and on seeing them set out in print their ludicrousness becomes manifest: for instance, 'yannanudder' – one another; 'dudta' – did thou, &c. It is not enough to enumerate the words believed to be purely Cumbrian. There are many contractions, corruptions, and combinations now current, which custom and time are gradually incorporating into the dialect, and which another generation or two will stamp as provincialisms; and without a key to such, a stranger would encounter many difficulties in ordinary conversation with an untravelled native,

A great variety of words are in common use expressive of the superlative or extraordinary; of beating or punishing; and of idiocy or weak-mindedness.

It is in these combinations, and other changes, that the connection of our dialect with other tongues is made apparent to the searcher into languages. For those reasons, the seeming redundancy of words in the following collection may be held excusable.

It is hardly necessary to apologise for any unseemly words which may be thought to occur: if any such are supposed to be found, it is it is equally certain they are requisite to complete the work, to the exclusion of more offensive terms.'

Excerpt from *A Glossary of the Words and Phrases of Cumberland* by WILLIAM DICKINSON, 1859

Inspiring writers

The Lake District has been a source of inspiration for many writers, dialect and otherwise.

Joseph Relph

JOSEPH (also known as *Josiah*) RELPH was a poet who wrote in the dialect of Cumberland in the 1700s. Relph was born in Churchtown and his father's estate was in the parish of Sebergham in Cumberland. Relph's dialect writings and other works were first published in 1747 as *A Miscellany of Poems*. Relph left Cumberland for Glasgow at an early age, but soon returned to become a teacher in his home village. He also took holy orders and became the curate of the parish of Sebergham. When Relph wasn't writing, he worked hard to help improve the lives of local people.

Horace, Book II, Ode VII
In the Cumberland dialect (extract)

> The snow has left the fells and fled,
> Their tops i green the trees hev' cled;
> The grund wi' sindry flowers is sown,
> And to their stint the becks are fawn;
> Nor fear the nymphs and graces mair
> To dance it in the meadows bare,
> The year, 'at slips sae fast away,
> Whispers we mun not think to stay:
> The spring suin thows the winter frost,
> To meet the spring does simmer post;
> Frae simmer autumn cleeks the hauld,
> And back at yence is winter cauld.

From *Poems, humorous and sentimental: consisting of Cumberland pastorals: translations and imitations from the classics; epistles, fables, songs, and epigrams* by JOSIAH RELPH, 1805

John Richardson
Cumbrian Image Bank

John Richardson

Born in 1817 at Stone Cottage in Naddle, near Keswick, JOHN RICHARDSON was to go on to create a body of poems and writings that captured the Cumberland dialect. To this day, his writing is known for its direct style and sense of humour. In 1871, Richardson published *Cummerland Talk: Being Short Tales and Rhymes in the Dialect of that County, Together With A Few Miscellaneous Pieces In Verse*. Richardson wasn't only known for his writing talents. This son of a dry stone waller was also a builder, having played a key role in helping to rebuild the church of his home village (in later life) of St-John's-in-the-Vale, as well as the neighbouring school and the vicarage.

It's Nobbut Me

Ya winter neet, I mind it weel,
Oor lads 'ed been at t' fell,
An', bein' tir't went seun to bed.
An' I sat be messel.

I hard a jike on t' window pane,
An' deftly went to see;
Bit when I ax't, 'Who's jiken theer?'
Says t' chap, 'It's nobbut me!'

'Who's me? says I, 'What want ye here?
Oor fwoak ur aw abed?'
'I dunnet want your fwok at aw,
It's thee I want,' he said.
'What can t'e want wi' me,' says I;
'An' who the deuce can 't be?
Just tell me who it is an' then'
Says he, 'It's nobbut me.'

Excerpt from *It's Nobbut Me* by JOHN RICHARDSON

The Cumberland Bard

ROBERT ANDERSON progressed from humble beginnings to bringing his native North Cumbrian dialect to life in songs and ballads, earning himself the title of 'The Cumberland Bard'. Anderson set his words to popular tunes, which made his work even more widespread. One of his ballads, *Barbary Bell*, became so popular that it led to the creation of a country dance of the same name!

Interestingly, a song that Anderson wrote about a young farm boy who joined the army grew popular along the Cumbrian coast, becoming in the process a song about a miner, *The Recruited Collier*. This then went on to become celebrated in the folk revival of the 20th century. It is said that Anderson featured people from his own life in his songs, which tended to make him more than a little paranoid!

The quality of Anderson's work was acknowledged by MELVYN BRAGG in the 1980s, who commented that Anderson's work is due for 'reclamation and discovery'. You can still view the memorial to Anderson at Carlisle Cathedral. It has the inscription *'Erected by public subscription to the memory of Robert Anderson, the Cumberland Bard, died in Carlisle, 26 Sept. 1833, aged 63 years'*. The centenary edition of *Anderson's Cumberland Ballads and Songs* was published in 1904.

Barbary Bell

(Tune - *Cuddle and cuddle us aw thegether*)
   O but this luive is a serious thing!
   It's the beginner o' monie waes;
   And yen had as guid in a helter swing,

As luik at a bonny feace now-a-days:
Was there ever peer deevil sae fash'd as me?
Nobbet sit your ways still, the truth I's tell,
For I wish I'd been hung on our codlen tree,
The varra furst time I seed Barbary Bell!

Excerpt from *Barbary Bell* by ROBERT ANDERSON, from *Ballads in the Cumberland Dialect*, 1870

The Muse of Cumberland

Born in 1747 near Cardew in Cumberland, SUSANNA BLAMIRE did not publish much work during her lifetime. The work that she did publish was done so anonymously. Three of these works ended up being set to music by JOSEPH HADYN. Blamire's work was acknowledged by no less than CHARLES DICKENS in *The Old Curiosity Shop* when he quoted the first two lines of *The Siller Croun!* Blamire's poems were collected in 1842, with a combination of poems in Cumberland dialect and in Scottish dialect.

It was then she went on to become known as '*The Muse of Cumberland*'. Blamire's reputation continued to grow long after her death and she is now thought to have had an influence on the work of ROBERT BURNS.

The Toiling Day His Task Has Duin

The toiling day his task has duin,
And night sits on yon mountain's brow,
She's luikt her last luik o' the sun,
An' muffl'd up the vales below.
The weary ploughman seeks his heaam,
His blythsome ingle far he sees;
An' oft peeps out his winsome deame,
While the wee things rin aroun' the bleeze.

Excerpt from *The Toiling Day His Task is Duin*, from *The Poetical Works of Miss Susanna Blamire*

Mary Powley

Apart from the fact that she was born in 1811 in Langwathby to a successful farming family, not a great deal is known about MARY POWLEY. What we do know is that Powley was both passionate about the past and about writing. Her talents were considerable, as suggested by the fact that she succeeded in translating several poems from Danish despite never having left her native Cumbria! Powley wrote some poems in her local dialect, as well as some more conventional Victorian pieces. She also wrote for the Transactions of the Cumberland and Westmorland Antiquarian and Archaeological Society as well as publishing *Echoes of Old Cumberland* in 1875.

Cumberland Thanksgiving Song

The blast frae dark fells o'er us,
That sweeps through Cumbria's vales,
Taks up the nation's chorus, —
God bless the Prince o' Wales!
Wi' voice o' beacons bleezin',
Lown breeze owre muirs an' cairns, —
God bless our Danish Princess!
God bless their bonny bairns!

Wi' London millions pourin'
For thanksgivin' an' prayers,
'The Queen!' — 'The Prince!' — implorin'
Blessin's on them an' theirs;
Thanksgivin'-Cumbrians gather —
For that spared royal life;
To the smaa bairns their father —
The husband to his wife.

Excerpt from *Echoes of Old Cumberland. Poems and translations* by MARY POWLEY, 1875

Alexander Craig Gibson

Born in 1813 in Harrington, Cumberland, ALEXANDER CRAIG GIBSON went on to become a doctor. However, he had been a keen writer to newspapers even when he was young.

His first book, *The Old Man, or Ravings and Ramblings round Coniston*, was printed in chapters in the *Kendal Mercury*. His writing career took on momentum after health problems led to his retirement. In 1873, Gibson published *The Folk-speech of Cumberland and some Districts adjacent, being Short Stories and Rhymes in the Dialect of the West Border Counties*. He was also a passionate about the past and was involved with antiquarian associations, writing for their journals and also for other journals on geology and related topics.

Keaty Curbison's Cat
An oald, oald stwory

> *Keaty Curbison's cat hed a whudderin' waow,*
> *A waow like a yowl, fit to freeten a man;*
> *An' t' leet iv it e'e was a green glentin' lowe —*
> *Iv it' e'e ^ we may say, for it no' but hed yan.*
>
> *T' ya lug hed been rowen an' hung like a cloot.*
> *While t' tudder stack up like t' cockad' iv a hat ;*
> *Lang whiskers like briissles spread o' roond it' snoot —*
> *It wosn't a beauty — Keaty Curbison's cat!*

Excerpt from *Keaty Curbison's Cat*, from *The Folk-speech of Cumberland and Some Districts Adjacent*, 1869

A Celebrated Dialect

The people of Cumbria and the Lake District are proud champions of their local dialects. The area has a long heritage of capturing and celebrating the words, language and pronunciation that is so unique to them. One important example of this is the thriving Lakeland Dialect Society. Going strong since 1939, not only is it active in celebrating past dialect and dialect writers, it also showcases local dialect writers of today.

It does this through regular meetings, special events and a long-running journal. The society also publishes work by current dialect writers and poets. It was also involved with running the very first National Dialect Day in Cumbria in 2014! You can find out more at **www. lakelanddialectsociety.org**.

Ethel Fisher

One writer who continues to keep the Cumbrian dialect alive to this day is ETHEL FISHER. A local of West Cumbria, Ethel has helped to capture the heritage and the voices of the area in her books. In *Old Fashioned Fairy Tales*, Ethel retells 14 traditional fairy tales in the contemporary West Cumbrian accent!

The author has also written *Humorous Tales in Cumberland Dialect Rhyme* and *More Humorous Tales in Cumberland Dialect Rhyme*. Ethel's achievements have been recognised with an MBE.

A name for local dialect

Yet another important name in the area's long history of dialect writing is that of LANCELOT SALKELD PORTER. Lancelot succeeded in producing a great deal of work in the local dialect, both poetry and prose. He also helped to found the Lakeland Dialect Society. In more recent times, the society has honoured Porter's achievements by publishing a book of his articles, poems and press cuttings.

Cumbria's rapping farmer

For another perspective on Cumbrian dialect, look no further than Cumbria's rapping farmer, DICKY DICKINSON! It's fair to say that his performance of *Dip me baby yan more time* is something that should be experienced. Dicky became an internet sensation after thousands of people watched his performances on YouTube.

Writers influenced by the Lake District

While the area has enjoyed a notable number of dialect champions, it has also inspired many other writers.

William
Wordsworth
Creative Commons

William Wordsworth

No exploration of writing and the Lake District would be complete without a mention of WILLIAM WORDSWORTH. It is testament to the power of the Lake District that even though Wordsworth did not move back to the land of his birth until later in life, he went on to be known as one of the 'Lake Poets'. In fact, he was one of the central figures of what went on to be known as the Lakes School, along with Samuel Taylor Coleridge and Robert Southey.

There is much more to Wordsworth's relationship with the Lake District than the famous daffodils. It was a tour of the Lake District with Coleridge which led to William and his sister Dorothy moving to Dove Cottage in Grasmere. You can now visit the cottage where Wordsworth wrote some of his best-known poems. You can even see the journal entry written by Dorothy Wordsworth that led to her brother writing about those daffodils! Dorothy and William moved to Allan Bank in Grasmere, then to the Old Rectory opposite St Oswald's Church. In 1813 they moved to Rydal Mount, where they stayed until their deaths. Did you know that this leading light of the Romantic poets became Distributor of Stamps for Westmorland while he was at Rydal Mount, with an office in Church Street in Ambleside? In 1820, Wordsworth published his *Guide through the District of the Lakes*. This book is thought to have helped to inspire the first wave of mass tourism in the Lake District, somewhat ironic considering that he was drawn to the area because of its beauty and serenity.

Following the death of ROBERT SOUTHEY in 1843, Wordsworth was offered the position of Poet Laureate, which he at first turned down due to his age. When the Prime Minister, ROBERT PEEL, assured him that *'nothing will be required of you'*, Wordsworth took up the role, resigning his role as Stamp Distributor! Indeed, he is the only Poet Laureate of England not to have produced a single verse of official poetry! But that didn't mean that he wasn't industrious. In his working life, Wordsworth wrote 70,000 lines of verse. That's 40,000 lines more than any other poet!

To this day, you can view Wordsworth's carved name in his school desk at Hawkshead Grammar School.

Going back to those famous daffodils, no one knows for sure the true location of those inspiring flowers, but many places compete for the honour, with the biggest contender thought to be somewhere between Patterdale and Gowbarrow by Ullswater.

While Wordsworth did not write in dialect, he challenged the poetic conventions of the time, fighting for a more natural voice. In his poem *Michael*, he aimed to speak in a 'rustic dialect'. While the effect of the local dialect is more subtle than in other writers we've looked at, Wordsworth's poetry captures a spirit of place which is undeniably the Lake District.

> *'A sort of national property in which every man has a right and interest who has an eye to perceive and a heart to enjoy.'*
WILLIAM WORDSWORTH on the Lake District

Beatrix Potter

Think of writers and the Lake District and the name of BEATRIX POTTER is bound to spring to mind. The area had a significant influence on Potter's charming and timeless stories of animals, which have entranced generations of children and adults alike. Potter's link with the Lake District began with a holiday stay at Wray Castle near Ambleside (interestingly, Potter's parents entertained many high-profile people there, including Hardwicke Rawnsley, the vicar of Low Wray Church who was to become one of the founders of the National Trust). The Potter family continued to enjoy holidays in the area, but it was after Potter began to earn an income from her *Peter Rabbit* books that she was able to buy Hill Top Farm in Near Sawrey. In 1909, Potter bought another farm opposite Hill Top, Castle Farm, which became her main Lake District base. Seven of Potter's books are based in or around Hill Top. Today it is the most visited literary spot in the Lake District!

Potter is famed for her talent for creating fictional animals, but did you know that she also had a significant impact on real-life animals in the Lake District? This was because she became a key figure in saving the area's traditional Herdwick sheep from extinction. Potter became an expert Herdwick sheep breeder and was the first woman to be elected president-designate of the Herdwick Sheep Breeders' Association, which continues to this day. When Potter died in 1943, she left 14 farms, herds of sheep and 4,000 acres of land to the National Trust.

Alfred Wainwright, MBE

If you're a keen walker, you'll already know what a 'Wainwright' is. For the rest of us, the Wainwrights are the 214 fells described in ALFRED WAINWRIGHT's seven-volume work, *A Pictorial Guide to the Lakeland Fells*. Alfred Wainwright (known affectionately as 'AW') MBE combined his love of the Lake District, fell walking, illustrating and writing to create a legacy which is still going strong to this day. In fact, more than two million copies of the Pictorial Guides have been sold worldwide since their first publication!

Arthur Ransome

The Lake District inspired and provide much of the setting for *Swallows and Amazons*, created by ARTHUR RANSOME. While Ransome was born in Leeds, he enjoyed his holidays in the area around Coniston and also went to school in Windermere. In his adult life, Ransome and his wife made their home in the Winster Valley and Haverthwaite, which is where Ransome wrote many of the Swallows and Amazons series. Interestingly, it was Ransome's connection with W.G. Collingwood, who worked as assistant and secretary to the writer John Ruskin, which was to nurture his relationship with the area in his adult life. This is because Collingwood's home was right beside Coniston Water, where Ransome learned to sail. Another important influence could well have been that the book which Ransome loved most in his childhood was Collingwood's Thorstein of the Mere, which was set around Coniston.

Postman Pat

It may surprise you to learn that the world's most famous fictional postie hails from Cumbria! The writer behind Postman Pat (and his black and white cat), JOHN CUNLIFFE, lived in Kendal for six years. Postman Pat's world of Greendale was inspired by nearby Longsleddale, while Greendale post office was based on Beast Banks post office in Kendal. Although the post office is sadly now closed, the connection is marked with a plaque on the building.

John Ruskin

It could be argued that the impact of this Victorian writer, artist and philosopher would not have been the same without the influence of the Lake District. Ruskin had powerful memories of his childhood visits to the area, once saying: *'The first thing which I remember as an event in my life was being taken by my nurse to the brow of Friar's Crag on Derwentwater.'*

Ruskin continued to visit the place throughout his life and eventually bought Brantwood, overlooking Coniston, retiring there in 1884. The house became a regular haunt for some of the greatest intellectuals and artists of the time such as Holman Hunt, Kate Greenaway and Charles Darwin.

Ruskin's influence continues to this day. He is recognised as having anticipated the greenhouse effect over one hundred years ago. He also helped to spark the establishment of The National Trust and the National Parks movement. Would any of this have been possible without his connection with the Lake District?

Counting sheep

What does counting sheep have to do with the language of Cumbria? Well, quite a lot, it seems. To this day, an oral tradition survives – a dialect number system of counting sheep. It is thought to be based on an approach derived from the Norse settlers when they came to the area. It seems that Cumbrian shepherds used the **Yan Tan Tethera** system in which they counted sheep in groups of twenty, then moved small stones between their pockets to keep a tally of the total. The count wouldn't exceed 20, because a stone was dropped for every group of 20 sheep counted. If there were more sheep, the count simply started again!

The Yan Tan Tethera system was popular among local shepherds right up until the Industrial Revolution. It was also once used for counting stitches in knitting.

Yan	Othera	Bumfit
Tyan	Dothera	Yanabumfit
Tethera	Deek	Tyanabumfit
Methera	Yandeek	Tetherabumfit
Pimp	Tyandeek	Metherabumfit
Sethera	Tetheradeek	Jiggit
Lethera	Metheradeek	

'The dialect of these two counties, it is said, changes with each mile, and the language is difficult of under-standing by people living six miles apart.'

From *A Bibliography of the Dialect Literature of Cumberland and Westmorland, and Lancashire North-of-the-Sands* by ARCHIBALD SPARKE, published 1907

'In the present work no attempt is made to explain or account for anything of a peculiar character in the dialect. If language grows out of life, we are justified in regarding ours as a type, and those who are most familiar with the life out of which it has grown, will be most likely those to regard it most leniently. They will know something of the social habits which the fair and market, the smithy hearth, the shoemaker's shop are dominating factors in forming. They will understand what it is to be concerned with cattle, and the elements, as others are with more mighty affairs. Out of the exigencies of ploughing, sowing, reaping, and gathering;

of boon days and ale days; of shiftings and settlings; of hiring and term times they know what to expect and will not be annoyed by grossness, or deterred by affectations or their absence.'

Excerpt from *Lakeland Words: A Collection of Dialect Words and Phrases, as Used in Cumberland and Westmorland* by B. KIRKBY, published 1898

Land of leisure?

On the map: outside Winster Post Office tourists prepare for their next walk Cumbria County Council; Kendal Library

What do you associate with Cumbria and the Lake District? Most of us think of picturesque rural scenery. Whether it's

Cumbria's rich history or its status as the largest national park in Britain, it's common to connect the place with Wordsworth, long walks, Wainwright and beautiful views. No wonder, with an area which contains the UK's most popular national park. Established in 1951 and covering 2,292 square kilometres (885 square miles), the Lake District features Scafell Pike, the highest mountain in England at 978 metres (3,209 feet) as well as over 6,000 archaeological sites and monuments, plus 1,740 buildings and 21 conservation areas. Many of us link the area with leisure time, if the 15 million visitors a year to the Lake District are anything to go by!

With picture postcard views that have been inspiring poets and others for centuries, it's not surprising that Cumbria and the Lake District are closely associated with pleasure and leisure. In fact, the holidaymakers who head for the Lake District these days might be surprised to learn that tourism in the area only started in the late eighteenth century. Before then, it wasn't seen as a particularly tempting destination. Cultural differences in how people viewed rural places in the past meant that early travellers to the area were not impressed, with a person no less august than Daniel Defoe writing about it in 1724 as: *'the wildest, most barren and frightful of any that I have passed over in England, or even Wales itself; the west side, which borders on Cumberland, is indeed bounded by a chain of almost unpassable mountains which, in the language of the country, are called fells.'*

William Wordsworth didn't just immortalise the Lake District in his poetry. He also helped to change the way people saw it in his day, particularly after the publication in 1820 of his guidebook A Guide through the District of the Lakes in the North of England. It proved to be hugely popular and brought more tourists into the area, going on to be produced in five volumes. Add to this better working conditions and the opening of the railway to Windermere and you have the ideal conditions for the first wave of tourism to the Lake District. While the railway opened up parts of the Lake District to people who had never been there before, it also helped to bring more visitors to others parts of Cumbria.

In 1951 the Lake District was granted national park status in order to protect the landscape by restricting development. The majority of the land is in private ownership, with small areas belonging to the National Trust. These days, the Lake District attracts as many tourist as London. That's not surprising, considering how much there is to explore, whether it is beautiful Windermere, historic Dove Cottage or Great Langdale in the Lakes or Carlisle Castle, Eden Valley or Hadrian's Wall (a UNESCO World Heritage site).

Lord Carlisle's railway in 1920 Denis Perriam

A history of industry

As you might expect, sheep farming was a big part of the history of the area. The breed which is literally part of the local landscape is the Herdwick. As you can discover elsewhere in this book, a great champion of the Herdwick was the writer Beatrix Potter. However, if you look beyond the essential traditional rural industries, you'll soon discover another side to Cumbria and the Lake District that is perhaps less well known.

A clue to the past:
the disused Head Gear
at Haig Pit Whitehaven
Mick Garratt

While it may not seem particularly romantic or picturesque, mining was once a major aspect of life in the Lake District and Cumbria, thanks to the rich resources hidden away under the picturesque scenery. Locals earned a living from the mining of copper, lead, slate and other materials. This long history pretty much ended in March 1986, when Haig Pit, Cumbria's last deep coal mine, finally closed. While mining is almost completely a thing of the past with just a few clues left in the landscape, a small amount does continue to this day in some areas. Another less well-known fact about the area is that it actually helped to establish the pencil industry, due to locally mined graphite, particularly in Keswick, which has its own pencil museum.

Another thing many people do not associate with the Lake District is bobbins. Yet in the 19th century the Lake District was supplying half the world's textile industry with bobbins!

The bobbin mill at Caldbeck with coppiced wood stacked up, in the 1900s Cumbrian Image Bank

While Cumbria may not be generally known for mining or industry today, look a little closer and you'll soon find that many major names are closely associated with the area. Carlisle is home to one of just two Pirelli tyre plants in the country. The city is also the base for the headquarters of major haulage business, The Stobart Group, while just beyond the city you'll find a Nestlé factory. Carr's Milling Industries plc, which is based in Carlisle, owns a factory at Silloth that makes the Carr's Breadmaker flour range and other products. The headquarters of world rally company, M-Sport is based near Cockermouth while at Siddick you'll find the only UK factory of Swedish paper maker, Iggesund Paperboard. Tata Steel owns a cast products plant at Workington. The shipyard at Barrow-in-Furness is one of the UK's largest, with BAE Systems as the current owner.

Bricklayers at work Cumbrian Image Bank

If you think the Lake District is just about the business of tourism you should think again. In Ulverston, the pharmaceutical giant, GlaxoSmithKline, has a major base. Windermere is the home of popular homeware chain Lakeland, while a subsidiary of the Heinz company, Farley Health Products, has a factory in Kendal.

For Sale?

In early 2015 the Lake District National Park Authority (LDNP) announced that it was putting a number of sites in the Lake District up for sale. The authority has had its budget cut by almost 23 per cent since 2010. It put seven properties on the market, including Stickle Tarn in Great Langdale; river frontage at Portinscale, Keswick; Blue Hill and Red Bank Wood at Ambleside; Blea Brows on the banks of Coniston Water at Torver; Baneriggs Wood between Grasmere and Rydal Water; and Lady Wood and White Moss, Grasmere. Not surprisingly, the news was greeted by shock in many places with local people seeking to form alliances and make bids. To date, just two of the eight properties have been sold. The authority is in talks with one community group and one charity. Meanwhile, a national petition to stop the sale is gaining traction. Whatever your view, the reality is that the Lake District will be continue to be affected by the concerns – commercial and otherwise – of the day, just as it always has been.

The Tizzie-Wizzie of Windermere

The **Tizzie-Wizzie** is the charming name of Lake Windermere's very own mythical creature! It's what you get if you combine the body of a hedgehog with the wings of a bee and the tail of a squirrel! This unusual animal was first seen by a boatman in Bowness in the 1900s. It is said to be fond of water, but very shy. In 1906, one Tizzie-Wizzie was captured and rushed to a photographic studio. However, it escaped just after the photo was taken! The boatmen in the area took visitors on Tizzie-Wizzie hunts, yet they never found any. One American visitor offered a £5 reward for the capture of the Tizzie-Wizzie, either dead or alive! Sightings of the Tizzie-Wizzie are still reported to this day…

The Lucks of Cumbria

When people talk about **'Luck'** in Cumbria, they may well be referring to objects which hold magical powers. Cumbria is the origin of 'Lucks' – drinking vessels thought to help protect a home from bad fortune. The most high-profile one is believed to be the Luck of Edenhall, a village near Langwathby in the Eden valley. The resident family, the Musgraves, were the proud possessors of the glass beaker which was beautifully designed with coloured enamel and gilding. Thought to be Egyptian or Syrian and dating back to the 13th or 14th century, one early Musgrave put the acquisition down to fairies! According to him, 'a party of Fairies were drinking and making merry round a well near the Hall, called St Cuthbert's well; but being interrupted by the intrusion of some curious people, they were frightened, and made a hasty retreat, and left the cup in question: one of the last screaming out:

'If this cup should break or fall
Farewell the Luck of Edenhall!'"

The Edenhall Luck has been in the care of the Victoria and Albert Museum since 1926. It outlived the house it came from, which was sadly demolished in 1934.

Land of legends

Cumbria's rich history has been connected with two fascinating figures that have been celebrated in many tales.

King Arthur

Cumbria has been long been associated with KING ARTHUR, with a number of local monuments and sites providing numerous possible links with Arthurian legend. One of these is the stone monument near Penrith called King

Arthur's Round Table. Sadly, given that the site pre-dates King Arthur by at least 2,500 years, it is unlikely to have any historical connections with him! Another location is Birdoswald Roman Fort, which has been suggested as the site of King Arthur's last battle, Camlann. A 12th-century castle near Kirkby Stephen is said to stand on the site of an earlier castle built by Arthur's father, UTHER PENDRAGON. Indeed the present castle has long been known as Pendragon's Castle. According to some stories, the wizard MERLIN derived his magic from the Castlerigg and Long Meg stone circles. Bassenthwaite Lake is often said to be the resting place of Arthur's sword EXCALIBUR. The poet ALFRED, LORD TENNYSON was inspired to write his poems *Morte d'Arthur* and *Idylls of the King* while staying in Mirehouse, overlooking the lake.

Adam Bell

ADAM BELL is Cumbria's own Robin Hood. Bell was an outlaw who made his home in the Inglewood Forest near Carlisle. The story goes that he and his men were outlawed for stealing game. After they were caught for some other misdemeanours, the King agreed to pardon them if Adam succeeded in shooting an apple on his son's head from a distance of 120 paces. Fortunately, Adam achieved it and earned the pardon of the king!

The irony of a name

The name **'Lake District'** is somewhat misleading. This is because there is actually only one body of water with the word 'lake' in its title in the entire area – Bassenthwaite Lake. This makes it the only official lake in the Lake District! Even the area's biggest lake, Windermere, is named after a different version of 'water' or 'lake' i.e. a 'mere'!

A popular setting

Even if you've never visited the Lake District, you'll probably recognise Helvellyn's Striding Edge. This stunning ridge with its nerve-inducing steep drops has been the background setting for many a film or TV programme. Some say it is probably the most recognised image of the Lake District!

Helvellyn iStock

Hardknott Roman Fort iStock

Hardknott Roman Fort

Cumbria is the home of the best-preserved Roman fort in the UK. Hardknott was built 260 metres (850 feet) above sea level, close to the Roman road which leads from the coast over the Hardknott and Wrynose passes. The Romans knew the fort by a different name: *Mediobogdum*.

A destination for romance

The Lake District is still a byword for romance, with the area voted the second most romantic destination in the UK in 2015. It was topped only by London in a survey conducted by the **Hotels.com website**, but has been voted the most romantic location of all in the past. However, the Lake District has recently been voted as the UK's most romantic place in which to propose!

A sanctuary for red squirrels

The Lake District is a major sanctuary for the red squirrel, having the largest population in England. The wider area of Cumbria is also an important habitat for the brightly coloured creatures, though sadly they are still at risk of extinction. There are 140,000 red squirrels in the UK compared with around 2.5 million grey squirrels.

Red Squirrel iStock

Lighting up the future

In contrast with the area's rural and romantic image, it actually led the way in the move towards modern comforts. Windermere and Bowness were the second part of England to have electric street lighting, the power for which was supplied by a hydro-electric plant at Troutbeck Bridge.

The deep freeze

In 1895, Lake Windermere was frozen over for six weeks, making it possible to walk from one side to the other. It also froze in 1864, 1946 and 1963.

Wonderful and woolly

Cumbria has long been proud of its native animal, the Cumbrian Herdwick sheep. They've proved to be an essential part of the landscape and, in older times, of local people's livelihoods, thanks to their strength and talent for surviving just on what they forage. Their wool has impressive qualities too, with their thick bristly fibres forming a protective layer in blizzards. Herdwicks have been known to survive under a blanket of snow for three days while eating their own wool! BEATRIX POTTER played an important role in helping this breed survive, as you can discover in another part of this book.

The Shepherd's Life

Yet another sign of the continuing fascination with the world of the Lake District is the public response to *The Shepherd's Life: A Tale of the Lake District* by JAMES REBANKS. Published in 2015, the book shares the true story of Rebanks's years as a sheep farmer on the north-eastern fells of the Lake District. As the eldest son in a sheep-farming family that has worked in the Lake District for no less than 600 years, Rebanks shares the realities of the shepherding life in today's Lake District. While keeping a long shepherding heritage alive, he is also well in tune with contemporary life, having more than 60,000 followers on Twitter!

Country cottages

The Lake District is known for its picturesque whitewashed cottages. Yet despite appearances, they weren't painted white to look pretty. That bright covering is actually a coating of limewash and red lead to help prevent damp from coming in. This isn't really surprising when you consider that the Lake District's location and geography make it the dampest part of England. Seathwaite is specifically the wettest inhabited place in the country, with average annual rainfall of 3,552mm.

Making tracks

The history of tourism in the Lake District is closely connected with the coming of the railways. The Kendal and Windermere Railway was the first railway to be built in the Lake District, coming to Kendal in 1846 and Windermere in 1847. The railway system was next extended to reach Coniston and Penrith, via Keswick and Cockermouth. The line to Lakeside in Windermere opened in 1869 to cater for the big wave of tourists.

The start of the National Trust

Look across Lake Windermere and you'll see the impressive pomp of **Wray Castle**. Created in 1840 for a retired surgeon from Liverpool, it was his relative, Hardwicke Rawnsley, who came up with the idea of creating a National Trust to help protect the countryside. Beatrix Potter enjoyed a holiday at Wray Castle in 1882 at the age of 16 and was also a keen conservationist. Today, a great deal of the land Potter once owned in the Lake District is the property of The National Trust.

Wray Castle David Bills

Lost and hound

Mystified by talk of **'hound trailing'** in Cumbria? It's a reference to a 200-year-old local tradition which brings together dogs and aniseed! In fact, it's one of Cumbria's oldest and most popular sports. Visit the area between April and October and you'll see hound trail racing all around the area. The specially trained hounds follow a strong aniseed and paraffin scent around a circular route of up to 10 miles. Each race can take from 25 to 40 minutes. Anyone wanting to participate in the running of hounds must be a member of the Hound Trailing Association and have their hounds registered.

England's highest

The Lake District is home to **Scafell Pike**, the highest mountain in England at 978 m (3,209 feet).

A presidential connection

It may surprise you to learn that Carlisle has a connection with a well-known US president. Woodrow Wilson's mother was actually born in the city. As a result, the president, who held office from 1913 to 1921, was a regular visitor to the city and surrounding area. In total, he made six visits to Cumbria. He visited Carlisle in December 1918 in what he called a 'pilgrimage of the heart'. This visit is commemorated by a plaque on one of the walls of Carlisle City Church on Lowther Street. Wilson's old family home is marked by a blue plaque from the Carlisle and District Civic Trust. His visit has also been commemorated with a pub named after him on Botchergate.

President Woodrow Wilson iStock

Carlisle's cursing stone

While Cumbria is associated with many pleasant things, it is also connected with something a little darker: a curse! **The curse of Carlisle** has been named by locals as the source of all kinds of problems, even today. In 1525, the Reivers of the borderlands had become such a danger to local communities that the then Archbishop of Glasgow, Gavin Dunbar, put a curse on all the Reivers: the Monition of Cursing. The thousand-word curse was duly proclaimed at every pulpit along the Scottish border.

Many years later, in 2001, a large stone inscribed with part of the curse was placed in the underpass near Carlisle's Tullie House Museum as part of Carlisle's Millennium Gateway scheme. Designed by local Carlisle artist, GORDON YOUNG and made by ANDY ALTMAN, it sits at the end of an 80-metre path which shows the names of all the Reiver families. Young himself is from an ancient Reiver family. The stone has since become infamous and associated with bad luck in the area such as foot and mouth disease, a flood, factory closures and sporting failures.

The rock carvings of William Mounsey

If you're out exploring the Lake District, you may encounter some unusual rock carvings. They are weird but fascinating and are the work of WILLIAM HENRY MOUNSEY. Born in 1808 into a family that lived in the Castletown Estate, Mounsey went on to live at Rockcliffe and became both an antiquarian and a soldier. He enjoyed exploring other cultures while visiting new countries. He also enjoyed making explorations in his local area. Mounsey created a monument at the source of the River Eden which was sadly destroyed by railway workers 20 years later.

The rock carvings of William Mounsey Creative Commons

A replica was set up in Outhgill in 1984. Mounsey was somewhat eccentric, inscribing 9th-century Welsh poetry on a pre-Roman site. He is believed to be the creator of **the five faces** (pictured on page 73) marked into the cliffs of Eden gorge, although there is still some controversy about their origins.

A taste of Cumbria and the Lake District

Cumberland Sausage

Cumberland's eponymous sausage is one of its most famous foodstuffs. Even though its history is thought to go back 500 years, the Cumberland sausage is still very much enjoyed today with its distinctive curled pattern still a staple of dinner plates across the country. To this day, no one really knows what inspired the sausage's well-known shape. Some think that it was simply a practical way to bring all the ingredients together while others believe it was inspired by the German miners living in Cumbria during Elizabeth I's reign, being the shape of sausages they were accustomed to enjoying at home. It's not just its quirky form that makes a Cumberland a little different from the average sausage. As well as being free from any added preservatives or colourings, the Cumberland sausage gains its chunkier texture from the fact the meat inside has been chopped rather than minced. In 2011, the sausage gained Protected

Geographical Indication status under EU law, which means that it can only be made in Cumbria! The sausage is all set to get its own festival too. Recently announced, the new annual Cumberland Sausage Festival celebrates all that's great about this local delicacy at Muncaster Castle on the Western Lake District!

A group out enjoying the countryside, perhaps with a sausage or two?
Cumbria Image Bank

Cumberland Ham

While there's no doubt that Cumbria is famed to this day for its delicious sausages, it would be unfair to overlook the Cumberland Ham. After all, both Cumberland and Westmorland have been famous for their hams for centuries! This is because of their flavour and long history. A traditional Cumberland Ham is dry-cured and made from the lower shank of a pig's hind leg. The ham is rubbed with salt, saltpetre, brown sugar or black treacle and dry-cured for one month. The rub is then washed off and the ham is air-dried for another two months. Over this period, the ham loses 20 per cent of its weight, which helps to make it even more flavoursome! While the ham used to be made from Cumberland pigs, these are now extinct, so it is now made from Middle White pigs. Like the sausage, chemical additives and preservatives are never used. One key point about the Cumberland Ham is that the traditional curing process preserves rather than cooks the ham, so you need to cook it before you eat it.

Cumberland Sauce

Confusingly, this sauce originally came from Germany! Created in the 19th century in Hanover in Germany, the sauce was named in honour of the Duke of Cumberland, who had links with the area. Nowadays, this fruity sauce is popular in Cumbria as well as being fondly enjoyed by many people across the country with meat such as ham, lamb and venison.

Try on a whig

If someone offers you a *'whig'* or a *'wigg'* in the Lake District, they're probably trying to give you something to eat rather than something to put on your head! A whig is a local type of slightly sweet bun. They were once baked in Lake District villages with each place having its own unique take on the tradition. These leavened buns were rather lighter and richer than household bread so were usually eaten as a special treat, with ale and cheese. Also referred to at times as *'arvel bread'*, whigs are believed to gain their name and purpose from Norse roots, having been an offering to the god, Wigga. However, another theory suggests that the name is taken from the Old German word for 'slice' or 'wedge'.

Kendal Mint Cake

No mention of food from the Lake District would be complete without a look at Kendal Mint Cake – the friend of many a keen walker! This highly energising confectionery proudly bears the name of its home of origin in Cumbria. Three companies still produce Kendal Mint Cake in Kendal. It was an essential part of the iron rations carried by EDMUND HILLARY and his team on the first successful ascent of Mount Everest in 1953.

Sources

DAVID CRYSTAL, *The Stories of English*, Penguin, 2004

www.newsandstar.co.uk/news/don-t-touch-carlisle-s-cursing-stone-it-ll-bring-us-bad-luck-football-fans-told-1.1098494

www.bbc.co.uk/cumbria/features/2003/07/restoration/the_curse.shtml

www.grough.co.uk/magazine/2015/03/21/trust-us-pleads-lake-district-boss-as-he-reveals-more-sell-offs-are-on-the-cards

www.itv.com/news/border/2015-03-13/thousands-object-to-lake-district-national-park-sale/

www.lakedistrict.gov.uk/learning/factstourism

www.funtrivia.com/en/subtopics/Carlisle-Cumbrias-Border-City-330916.html

www.independent.co.uk/travel/least-romantic-destination-in-britain-revealed-10024495.html

www.thewestmorlandgazette.co.uk/news/11879391.Lake_District_voted_most_romantic_place_to_propose_in_UK/

www.bbc.co.uk/cumbria/content/articles/2008/06/18/cumberland_lucks_june08_feature.shtml

www.vam.ac.uk/content/articles/t/the-luck-of-edenhall-history-and-myths/

http://mudcat.org/thread.cfm?threadid=11483

www.lakedistrict.gov.uk

www.visitcumbria.com

www.cwherald.com/a/archive/cumbrian-dialect-writer-remembered.254458.html

www.whitehavennews.co.uk/the-lost-bard-1.505017

www.visiteden.co.uk/explore-eden/

www.newsandstar.co.uk/features/people/cumbria-s-rapping-farmer-is-an-internet-sensation-1.837709

www.newsandstar.co.uk/features/was_king_arthur_s_round_table_in_cumbria_1_518847?referrerPath=home

http://thelakedistrict.info/lake-district-myths-and-legends/

Available now

Black Country Dialect

Bristol Dialect

Cockney Dialect

Cornish Dialect

Derbyshire Dialect

Devon Dialect

Dorset Dialect

Essex Dialect

Evolving English WordBank

Glaswegian Dialect

Hampshire Dialect

Kentish Dialect

Lancashire Dialect

Liverpool Dialect

Manchester Dialect

Newcastle upon Tyne Dialect

Norfolk Dialect

Nottinghamshire Dialect

Scottish Dialects

Somerset Dialect

Suffolk Dialect

Sussex Dialect

Warwickshire Dialect

Wiltshire Dialect

Yorkshire Dialect

Coming in 2015

Co Durham Dialect

Gloucestershire Dialect

Lincolnshire Dialect

Leicestershire Dialect

Welsh Borders Dialect

See website for more details: bradwellbooks.com